Meditations in an Emergency

Frank O'Hara

Meditations in an Emergency

Grove Press

New York

Some of these poems have appeared in: *A City Winter and Other Poems* (Tibor de Nagy Gallery Editions), *Partisan Review, Folder, Accent, New World Writing, Poetry,* and *The New American Poetry* (Grove Press, Inc).

Published simultaneously in Canada
Printed in the United States of America

Library of Congress Catalog Card Number 57-5136

ISBN 978-0-8021-3452-3

Second Edition, 1967

Grove Press
an imprint of Grove/Atlantic, Inc.
154 West 14th Street
New York, NY 10011

Distributed by Publishers Group West

www.groveatlantic.com

15 16 17 18   15 14 13 12

Contents

To Jane Freilicher

To the Harbormaster

I wanted to be sure to reach you;
though my ship was on the way it got caught
in some moorings. I am always tying up
and then deciding to depart. In storms and
at sunset, with the metallic coils of the tide
around my fathomless arms, I am unable
to understand the forms of my vanity
or I am hard alee with my Polish rudder
in my hand and the sun sinking. To
you I offer my hull and the tattered cordage
of my will. The terrible channels where
the wind drives me against the brown lips
of the reeds are not all behind me. Yet
I trust the sanity of my vessel; and
if it sinks, it may well be in answer
to the reasoning of the eternal voices,
the waves which have kept me from reaching you.

Poem

The eager note on my door said "Call me,
call when you get in!" so I quickly threw
a few tangerines into my overnight bag,
straightened my eyelids and shoulders, and

headed straight for the door. It was autumn
by the time I got around the corner, oh all
unwilling to be either pertinent or bemused, but
the leaves were brighter than grass on the sidewalk!

Funny, I thought, that the lights are on this late
and the hall door open; still up at this hour, a
champion jai-alai player like himself? Oh fie!
for shame! What a host, so zealous! And he was

there in the hall, flat on a sheet of blood that
ran down the stairs. I did appreciate it. There are few
hosts who so thoroughly prepare to greet a guest
only casually invited, and that several months ago.

To the Film Industry in Crisis

Not you, lean quarterlies and swarthy periodicals
with your studious incursions toward the pomposity of ants,
nor you, experimental theatre in which Emotive Fruition
is wedding Poetic Insight perpetually, nor you,
promenading Grand Opera, obvious as an ear (though you
are close to my heart), but you, Motion Picture Industry,
it's you I love!

In times of crisis, we must all decide again and again
    whom we love.
And give credit where it's due: not to my starched nurse,
    who taught me
how to be bad and not bad rather than good (and has
    lately availed
herself of this information), not to the Catholic Church
which is at best an over-solemn introduction to cosmic
    entertainment,
not to the American Legion, which hates everybody, but
    to you,
glorious Silver Screen, tragic Technicolor, amorous
    Cinemascope,
stretching Vistavision and startling Stereophonic Sound,
    with all
your heavenly dimensions and reverberations and
    iconoclasms! To
Richard Barthelmess as the "tol'able" boy barefoot and
    in pants,
Jeanette MacDonald of the flaming hair and lips and long,
    long neck,

Sue Carroll as she sits for eternity on the damaged fender
  of a car
and smiles, Ginger Rogers with her pageboy bob like a
  sausage
on her shuffling shoulders, peach-melba-voiced Fred Astaire
  of the feet,
Eric Von Stroheim, the seducer of mountain-climbers'
  gasping spouses,
the Tarzans, each and every one of you (I cannot bring
  myself to prefer
Johnny Weissmuller to Lex Barker, I cannot!), Mae West
  in a furry sled,
her bordello radiance and bland remarks, Rudolph Valentino
  of the moon,
its crushing passions, and moon-like, too, the gentle
  Norma Shearer,
Miriam Hopkins dropping her champagne glass off Joel
  McCrea's yacht
and crying into the dappled sea, Clark Gable rescuing
  Gene Tierney
from Russia and Allan Jones rescuing Kitty Carlisle from
  Harpo Marx,
Cornel Wilde coughing blood on the piano keys while
  Merle Oberon berates,
Marilyn Monroe in her little spike heels reeling through
  Niagara Falls,
Joseph Cotten puzzling and Orson Welles puzzled and
  Dolores del Rio
eating orchids for lunch and breaking mirrors, Gloria
  Swanson reclining,
and Jean Harlow reclining and wiggling, and Alice Faye
  reclining

and wiggling and singing, Myrna Loy being calm and wise,
    William Powell
in his stunning urbanity, Elizabeth Taylor blossoming, yes,
    to you

and to all you others, the great, the neargreat, the
    featured, the extras
who pass quickly and return in dreams saying your one
    or two lines,
my love!
Long may you illumine space with your marvellous
    appearances, delays
and enunciations, and may the money of the world
    glitteringly cover you
as you rest after a long day under the kleig lights with
    your faces
in packs for our edification, the way the clouds come often
    at night
but the heavens operate on the star system. It is a divine
    precedent
you perpetuate! Roll on, reels of celluloid, as the great
    earth rolls on!

Poem

At night Chinamen jump
on Asia with a thump

while in our willful way
we, in secret, play

affectionate games and bruise
our knees like China's shoes.

The birds push apples through
grass the moon turns blue,

these apples roll beneath
our buttocks like a heath

full of Chinese thrushes
flushed from China's bushes.

As we love at night
birds sing out of sight,

Chinese rhythms beat
through us in our heat,

the apples and the birds
move us like soft words,

we couple in the grace
of that mysterious race.

Blocks

1

Yippee! she is shooting in the harbor! he is jumping
up to the maelstrom! she is leaning over the giant's
cart of tears which like a lava cone let fall to fly
from the cross-eyed tantrum-tousled ninth grader's
splayed fist is freezing on the cement! he is throwing
up his arms in heavenly desperation, spacious Y of his
tumultuous love-nerves flailing like a poinsettia in
its own nailish storm against the glass door of the
cumulus which is withholding her from these divine
pastures she has filled with the flesh of men as stones!
O fatal eagerness!

2

O boy, their childhood was like so many oatmeal cookies.
I need you, you need me, yum, yum. Anon it became
    suddenly

3

like someone always losing something and never
    knowing what.
Always so. They were so fond of eating bread and
    butter and
sugar, they were slobs, the mice used to lick the floorboards
after they went to bed, rolling their light tails against

the rattling marbles of granulation. Vivo! the dextrose
those children consumed, lavished, smoked, in their knobby
candy bars. Such pimples! such hardons! such moody loves.
And thus they grew like giggling fir trees.

Les Etiquettes jaunes

I picked up a leaf
today from the sidewalk.
This seems childish.

Leaf! you are so big!
How can you change your
color, then just fall!

As if there were no
such thing as integrity!

You are too relaxed
to answer me. I am too
frightened to insist.

Leaf! don't be neurotic
like the small chameleon.

Aus einem April

We dust the walls.
And of course we are weeping larks
falling all over the heavens with our shoulders clasped
in someone's armpits, so tightly! and our throats are full.
Haven't you ever fallen down at Christmas
and didn't it move everyone who saw you?
isn't that what the tree means? the pure pleasure
of making weep those whom you cannot move by your flights!
It's enough to drive one to suicide.
And the rooftops are falling apart like the applause

of rough, long-nailed, intimate, roughened-by-kisses, hands.
Fingers more breathless than a tongue laid upon the lips
in the hour of sunlight, early morning, before the mist rolls
in from the sea; and out there everything is turbulent and green.

River

Whole days would go by, and later their years,
while I thought of nothing but its darkness
drifting like a bridge against the sky.
Day after day I dreamily sought its melancholy,
its searchings, its soft banks enfolded me,
and upon my lengthening neck its kiss
was murmuring like a wound. My very life
became the inhalation of its weedy ponderings
and sometimes in the sunlight my eyes,
walled in water, would glimpse the pathway
to the great sea. For it was there I was being borne.
Then for a moment my strengthening arms
would cry out upon the leafy crest of the air
like whitecaps, and lightning, swift as pain,
would go through me on its way to the forest,
and I'd sink back upon that brutal tenderness
that bore me on, that held me like a slave
in its liquid distances of eyes, and one day,
though weeping for my caresses, would abandon me,
moment of infinitely salty air! sun fluttering
like a signal! upon the open flesh of the world.

Poem

to James Schuyler

There I could never be a boy,
though I rode like a god when the horse reared.
At a cry from mother I fell to my knees!
there I fell, clumsy and sick and good,
though I bloomed on the back of a frightened black mare
who had leaped windily at the start of a leaf
and she never threw me.

I had a quick heart
and my thighs clutched her back.
I loved her fright, which was against me
into the air! and the diamond white of her forelock
which seemed to smart with thoughts as my heart smarted
    with life!
and she'd toss her head with the pain
and paw the air and champ the bit, as if I were Endymion
and she, moon-like, hated to love me.

All things are tragic
when a mother watches!
and she wishes upon herself
the random fears of a scarlet soul, as it breathes in and out
and nothing chokes, or breaks from triumph to triumph!

I knew her but I could not be a boy,
for in the billowing air I was fleet and green
riding blackly through the ethereal night
towards men's words which I gracefully understood,

and it was given to me
as the soul is given the hands
to hold the ribbons of life!
as miles streak by beneath the moon's sharp hooves
and I have mastered the speed and strength which is the
    armor of the world.

On Rachmaninoff's Birthday

Blue windows, blue rooftops
and the blue light of the rain,
these contiguous phrases of Rachmaninoff
pouring into my enormous ears
and the tears falling into my blindness

for without him I do not play,
especially in the afternoon
on the day of his birthday. Good
fortune, you would have been
my teacher and I your only pupil

and I would always play again.
Secrets of Liszt and Scriabin
whispered to me over the keyboard
on unsunny afternoons! and growing
still in my stormy heart.

Only my eyes would be blue as I played
and you rapped my knuckles,
dearest father of all the Russias,
placing my fingers
tenderly upon your cold, tired eyes.

The Hunter

He set out and kept hunting
and hunting. Where, he thought
and thought, is the real chamois?
and can I kill it where it is?
He had brought with him only a dish
of pears. The autumn wind soared
above the trails where the drops
of the chamois led him further.
The leaves dropped around him
like pie-plates. The stars fell
one by one into his eyes and burnt.

There is a geography which holds
its hands just so far from the breast
and pushes you away, crying so.
He went on to strange hills where
the stones were still warm from feet,
and then on and on. There were clouds
at his knees, his eyelashes
had grown thick from the colds,
as the fur of the bear does
in winter. Perhaps, he thought, I am
asleep, but he did not freeze to death.

There were little green needles
everywhere. And then manna fell.
He knew, above all, that he was now
approved, and his strength increased.
He saw the world below him, brilliant

as a floor, and steaming with gold,
with distance. There were occasionally
rifts in the cloud where the face
of a woman appeared, frowning. He
had gone higher. He wore ermine.
He thought, why did I come? and then,
I have come to rule! The chamois came.

The chamois found him and they came
in droves to humiliate him. Alone,
in the clouds, he was humiliated.

For Grace, After a Party

You do not always know what I am feeling.
Last night in the warm spring air while I was
blazing my tirade against someone who doesn't
interest
      me, it was love for you that set me
afire,
      and isn't it odd? for in rooms full of
strangers my most tender feelings
                    writhe and
bear the fruit of screaming. Put out your hand,
isn't there
      an ashtray, suddenly, there? beside
the bed? And someone you love enters the room
and says wouldn't
      you like the eggs a little
different today?
      And when they arrive they are
just plain scrambled eggs and the warm weather
is holding.

On Looking at "La Grande Jatte,"
the Czar Wept Anew

1

He paces the blue rug. It is the end of summer,
the end of his excursions in the sun. He
may now close his eyes as if they were tired flowers
and feel no sense of duty towards the corridor,
the recherché, the trees; they are all on his face,
a lumpy portrait, a painted desert. He is crying.
Only a few feet away the grass is green, the rug
he sees is grass; and people fetch each other in
and out of shadows there, chuckling and symmetrical.

The sun has left him wide-eyed and alone, hysterical
for snow, the blinding bed, the gun. "Flowers, flowers,
flowers!" he sneers, and echoes fill the spongy trees.
He cannot, after all, walk up the wall. The skylight
is sealed. For why? for a change in the season,
for a refurbishing of the house. He wonders if,
when the music is over, he should not take down
the drapes, take up the rug, and join his friends
out there near the lake, right here beside the lake!
"O friends of my heart!" and they will welcome him
with open umbrellas, fig bars, handmade catapults!
Despite the card that came addressed to someone else,
the sad fisherman of Puvis, despite his own precious
ignorance and the wild temper of the people, he'll try!

2

Now, sitting in the brown satin chair,
he plans a little meal for friends. So!
the steam rising from his Pullman kitchen
fogs up all memories of Seurat, the lake,
the summer; these are over for the moment,
beyond the guests, the cooking sherry and
the gin; such is the palate for sporadic
chitchat and meat. But as the cocktail
warms his courageous cockles he lets
the dinner burn, his eyes widen with
sleet, like a cloudburst fall the summer,
the lake and the voices! He steps into
the mirror, refusing to be anyone else,
and his guests observe the waves break.

3

He must send a telegram from the Ice Palace,
although he knows the muzhiks don't read:
"If I am ever to find these trees meaningful
I must have you by the hand. As it is, they
stretch dusty fingers into an obscure sky,
and the snow looks up like a face dirtied
with tears. Should I cry out and see what happens?
There could only be a stranger wandering
in this landscape, cold, unfortunate, himself
frozen fast in wintry eyes." Explicit Rex.

Romanze, or The Music Students

1

The rain, its tiny pressure
on your scalp, like ants
passing the door of a tobacconist.
"Hello!" they cry, their noses
glistening. They are humming
a scherzo by Tcherepnin.
They are carrying violin cases.
With their feelers knitting
over their heads the blue air,
they appear at the door of
the Conservatory and cry "Ah!"
at the honey of its outpourings.
They stand in the street and hear
the curds drifting on the top
of the milk of Conservatory doors.

2

They had thought themselves
in Hawaii when suddenly the pines,
trembling with nightfulness,
shook them out of their sibyllance.
The surf was full of outriggers
racing like slits in the eye of
the sun, yet the surf was full
of great black logs plunging, and
then the surf was full of needles.

The surf was bland and white,
as pine trees are white when,
in Paradise, no wind is blowing.

3

In Ann Arbor on Sunday afternoon
at four-thirty they went to an organ
recital: Messiaen, Hindemith, Czerny.
And in their ears a great voice said
"To have great music we must commission
it. To commission great music
we must have great commissioners."
There was a blast! and summer was over.

4

Rienzi! A rabbit is sitting in the hedge!
it is a brown stone! it is the month
of October! it is an orange bassoon!
They've been standing on this mountain
for forty-eight hours without flinching.
Well, they are soldiers, I guess,
and it is all marching magnificently by.

The Three-Penny Opera

I think a lot about
the Peachums: Polly
and all the rest are
free and fair. Her jewels
have price tags in case
they want to change
hands, and her pets
are carnivorous. Even
the birds.
   Whenever our
splendid hero Mackie
Messer, what an honest
man! steals or kills, there
is meaning for you! Oh
Mackie's knife has a false
handle so it can express
its meaning as well as
his. Mackie's not one to
impose his will. After all
who does own any thing?

But Polly, are you a
shadow? Is Mackie projected
to me by light through film?
If I'd been in Berlin in
1930, would I have seen you
ambling the streets like
Krazy Kat?
   Oh yes. Why,

when Mackie speaks we
only know what he means
occasionally. His sentence
is an image of the times.
You'd have seen all of us
masquerading. Chipper; but
not so well arranged. Air-
ing old poodles and pre-war
furs in narrow shoes
with rhinestone bows.
Silent, heavily perfumed.
Black around the eyes. You
wouldn't have known who
was who, though. Those
were intricate days.

A Terrestrial Cuckoo

What a hot day it is! for
Jane and me above the scorch
of sun on jungle waters to be
paddling up and down the Essequibo
in our canoe of war-surplus gondola parts.

We enjoy it, though: the bats squeak
in our wrestling hair, parakeets
bungle lightly into gorges of blossom,
the water's full of gunk and
what you might call waterlilies if you're

silly as we. Our intuitive craft
our striped T shirts and shorts
cry out to vines that are feasting
on flies to make straight the way
of tropical art. "I'd give a lempira or two

to have it all slapped onto a
canvas" says Jane. "How like
lazy flamingos look the floating
weeds! and the infundibuliform
corolla on our right's a harmless Charybdis!

or am I seduced by its ambient
mauve?" The nose of our vessel sneezes
into a bundle of amaryllis, quite
artificially tied with ribbon.
Are there people nearby? and postcards?

24

We, essentially travellers, frown
and backwater. What will the savages
think if our friends turn up? with
sunglasses and cuneiform decoders!
probably. Oh Jane, is there no more frontier?

We strip off our pretty blazers
of tapa and dive like salamanders
into the vernal stream. Alas! they
have left the jungle aflame, and in
friendly chatter of Kotzebue and Salonika our

friends swiftly retreat downstream
on a flowery float. We strike through
the tongues and tigers hotly, towards
orange mountains, black taboos, dada!
and clouds. To return with absolute treasure!

our only penchant, that. And a red-
billed toucan, pointing t'aurora highlands
and caravanserais of junk, cries out
"New York is everywhere like Paris!
go back when you're rich, behung with lice!"

Jane Awake

The opals hiding in your lids
    as you sleep, as you ride ponies
mysteriously, spring to bloom
    like the blue flowers of autumn

each nine o'clock. And curls
    tumble languorously towards
the yawning rubber band, tan,
    your hand pressing all that

riotous black sleep into
    the quiet form of daylight
and its sunny disregard for
    the luminous volutions, oh!

and the budding waltzes
    we swoop through in nights.
Before dawn you roar with
    your eyes shut, unsmiling,

your volcanic flesh hides
    everything from the watchman,
and the tendrils of dreams
    strangle policemen running by

too slowly to escape you,
    the racing vertiginous waves
of your murmuring need. But
    he is day's guardian saint

that policeman, and leaning
	from your open window you ask
him what dress to wear and how
	to comb your hair modestly,

for that is now your mode.
	Only by chance tripping on stairs
do you repeat the dance, and
	then, in the perfect variety of

subdued, impeccably disguisèd,
	white black pink blue saffron
and golden ambiance, do we find
	the nightly savage, in a trance.

A Mexican Guitar

Actors with their variety of voices
and nuns, those arch campaign-managers,
were pacing the campo in contrasting colors
as Jane and I muttered a red fandango.

A cloud flung Jane's skirt in my face
and the neighborhood boys saw such sights
as mortal eyes are usually denied. Arabian day!
she clicked her rhinestone heels! vistas of lace!

Our shouting knocked over a couple of palm trees
and the gaping sky seemed to reel at our mistakes,
such purple flashing insteps and careers!
which bit with lavish envy the northern soldiers.

Then loud startling deliberation! Violet peered,
hung with silver trinkets, from an adobe slit,
escorted by a famished movie star, beau idéal!
crooning that dejected ballad, *Anne the Strip*.

"Give me back my mink!" our Violet cried
"and cut out the heroics! I'm from Boston, remember."
Jane and I plotz! what a mysteriosabelle!
the fandango died on our lips, a wintry fan.

And all that evening eating peanut paste and onions
we chattered, sad, of films and the film industry
and how ballet is dying. And our feet ached. Violet
burst into tears first, she is always in the nick of time.

Chez Jane

The white chocolate jar full of petals
swills odds and ends around in a dizzying eye
of four o'clocks now and to come. The tiger,
marvellously striped and irritable, leaps
on the table and without disturbing a hair
of the flowers' breathless attention, pisses
into the pot, right down its delicate spout.
A whisper of steam goes up from that porcelain
eurythra. "Saint-Saëns!" it seems to be whispering,
curling unerringly around the furry nuts
of the terrible puss, who is mentally flexing.
Ah be with me always, spirit of noisy
contemplation in the studio, the Garden
of Zoos, the eternally fixed afternoons!
There, while music scratches its scrofulous
stomach, the brute beast emerges and stands,
clear and careful, knowing always the exact peril
at this moment caressing his fangs with
a tongue given wholly to luxurious usages;
which only a moment before dropped aspirin
in this sunset of roses, and now throws a chair
in the air to aggravate the truly menacing.

Two Variations

Suddenly that body appears: in my smoke
while someone's heavily describing Greece,
that famous monotonous line feels white
against the tensile gloom of life
and I seem intimate with what I merely touch.

1

Now I am not going to face things
because I am not a start
nor fall asleep against a heart
that doesn't burn the wolves away,
hunting and virtue beside an open fire.
And you know if I drift into the sky
it will be heavy as surf.

2

I'm glad that the rock is heavy
and that it feels all right in my heart
like an eye in a pot of humus.
Let's write long letters on grand themes,
fish sandwiches, egg sandwiches and cheese;
or travelling in Mexico, Italy and Australia.
I eat a lot so I won't get drunk and then
I drink a lot so I'll feel excited
and then I've gone away I don't know where
or with whom and can't remember whom from
except that I'm back with my paper bag
and next time my face won't come with me.

Ode

An idea of justice may be precious,
one vital gregarious amusement . . .

What are you amused by? a crisis
like a cow being put on the payroll
with the concomitant investigations and divinings?
Have you swept the dung from the tracks?
    Am I a door?
If millions criticize you for drinking too much,
the cow is going to look like Venus and you'll make a pass
yes, you and your friend from High School,
the basketball player whose black eyes exceed yours
as he picks up the ball with one hand.
    But doesn't he doubt, too?

    To be equal? it's the worst!
    Are we just muddy instants?

No, you must treat me like a fox; or, being a child,
kill the oriole though it reminds you of me.
Thus you become the author of all being. Women
    unite against you.

It's as if I were carrying a horse on my shoulders
and I couldn't see his face. His iron legs
hang down to the earth on either side of me
like the arch of triumph in Washington Square.
I would like to beat someone with him
but I can't get him off my shoulders, he's like evening.

Evening! your breeze is an obstacle,
    it changes me, I am being arrested,
    and if I mock you into a face
and, disgusted, throw down the horse—ah! there's his face!
and I am, sobbing, walking on my heart.

    I want to take your hands off my hips
    and put them on a statue's hips;

then I can thoughtfully regard the justice of your feelings
for me, and, changing, regard my own love for you
as beautiful. I'd never cheat you and say "It's inevitable!"
    It's just barely natural.
    But we do course together
like two battleships maneuvering away from the fleet.
I am moved by the multitudes of your intelligence
and sometimes, returning, I become the sea—
in love with your speed, your heaviness and breath.

Invincibility

"In the church of my heart the choir is on fire!"
—*Vladimir Mayakovsky*

1

Avarice, the noose that lets oil, oh my dear oh
"La Ronde," erase what is assured and ours, it
resurrects nothing, finally, in its eagerness
to sit under the widely spaced stairs, to be a fabulous
toilette, doesn't imitate footsteps of disappearance

The neighbor, having teased peace to retire, soon
averages six flowering fountains, ooh! spare the men
and their nervous companions that melt and ripen
into a sordid harbor of squid-slipping tarpaulin strips,
quits the sordid arbor of community butchers' girth

The jumping error pins hate on the blossoms of baffles,
densely foraging covered hero-Nero of Maltese, of Moor,
leap, oh leap! against the fame that's in the noose,
sister of yearning, of eclogues without overcoats deeply,
and the trumpet rages over the filigreed prisoners

Now sallies forth the joyousness of being cruel
which is singing of the world needed by the paralyzed wind,
seated and rebeginning, mounting without saying adieu,
never again delicately to entomb a tear,
that mark of suffering in the toughness of the forest

Lepers nest on the surly cats of glistening delirium,
feet of fire drowning in the attitude of relinquishing
    foreheads
remember always the barriers so cupiditously defended,
no spume breezy enough for the tempestuous sabers
sent reeling into the charades of fears of the nubile

A crisis questions its attendant in the eyelid of Verona
so serious are the lassitudes of a heart turned into a choir
and the fire-escapes tend to ferment against the paynim
    cheek
of love that's advancing into a maelstrom for a true speech,
succoring the lewd paupers deliberately, spear-like,
the pearl hesitating to come near the arid well

Noose arriving tropically masterful, estimating and caught,
let the crouching ferns release their nascent sonata
and, shaking with a remuneration of flaccid countries,
eat the rum that cruises an immortally non-sequitur finish,
quaint, and having an aspiration as of torrents and cars

Touched by the insensitivity that broods over the boats,
oh halos of startling carpets, canoes and lathes! archers!
a January of feeling seats itself before the young soldiers
and laughs and laughs at those arch-guardians' radiance,
particularly the sneer of fate, habit shaking its white fists

2

Now for some hell, you make a few fast purchases
separated by first nights of yoyo-cartwheel-violences,
ill but yelling and running full of the younger luminosity,

34

soulful, oh and epic and sort of rouged between the
    shoulder blades!
which the striding has not succeeded in making a gondola
    yet
and this has so devastated the murmuring contributions of
    strangers
in suits under the brilliant heather, although, my soul! it's
    white
it's painted white as the rain! and have you not taught
    for clarity,
for that sweet sake, the wordly dream of the son
    marching outward
always? and whispering of sins in the green clouds

An eagerness for the historical look of the mirror,
the dry smile of knowledge which is faithlessness
    apologizing
to the Sphinx, and is it not a great fury of horsemen
who make a guided tour of the future and its glass-like
    tortures?
the odor of evening vibrating across that linear nostalgia
and vouchsafing a plume and a volume of Plato,
purblind water, the earth pitting its stench against the
    moon's
and accomplishing a serenade, a terrestrial touchdown sigh
in the silence which is not yet formidable or ominous,
resenting the leaves and not yet geared to the undercutting
    foam

Poem in January

March, the fierce! like a wind of garters
its calm kept secret, as if eaten!
and sipped at the source tainted, taut.

Vagrants, crushed by such effulgence,
wrap their mild twigs and bruises in straws
and touch themselves tightly, like buttered bees,

for the sun is cold, there, as an eyeglass
playing with its freshly running sinuses,
swampy, and of a molasses sweetness on the cheek.

Turn, oh turn! your pure divining rod
for the sake of infantile suns and their railing
and storming at the deplorably pale cheeks

and the hemlocks not yet hung up.
Do we live in old, sane, sensible cries?
The guards stand up and down like a waltz

and its strains are stolen by fauns
with their wounded feet nevertheless dashing
away through the woods, for the iris! for autumn!

Oh pure blue of a footstep, have you stolen
March? and, with your cupiditous baton
struck agog? do you feel that you have, blue?

Ah, March! you have not decided whom you train.
Or what traitors are waiting for you to be born,
oh March! or what it will mean in terms of diet.

36

Take my clear big eyes into your heart, and then
pump my clear big eyes through your bloodstream, and!
stick my clear big eyes on your feet, it is cold,

I am all over snowshoes and turning round
and round. There's a trail of blood through
the wood and a few shreds of faun-colored hair.

I am troubled as I salute the crocus.
There shall be no more reclining on the powdered roads,
your veins are using up the redness of the world.

Meditations in an Emergency

Am I to become profligate as if I were a blonde? Or religious as if I were French?

Each time my heart is broken it makes me feel more adventurous (and how the same names keep recurring on that interminable list!), but one of these days there'll be nothing left with which to venture forth.

Why should I share you? Why don't you get rid of someone else for a change?

I am the least difficult of men. All I want is boundless love.

Even trees understand me! Good heavens, I lie under them, too, don't I? I'm just like a pile of leaves.

However, I have never clogged myself with the praises of pastoral life, nor with nostalgia for an innocent past of perverted acts in pastures. No. One need never leave the confines of New York to get all the greenery one wishes—I can't even enjoy a blade of grass unless I know there's a subway handy, or a record store or some other sign that people do not totally *regret* life. It is more important to affirm the least sincere; the clouds get enough attention as it is and even they continue to pass. Do they know what they're missing? Uh huh.

My eyes are vague blue, like the sky, and change all the time; they are indiscriminate but fleeting, entirely specific and disloyal, so that no one trusts me. I am always looking away. Or again at something after it has given me up. It makes me restless and that makes me unhappy, but I cannot keep them still. If only I had grey, green, black, brown, yellow eyes; I would stay at home and do something. It's not that I'm curious. On the contrary, I am bored but it's my duty to be attentive, I am needed by things as the sky must be above the earth. And lately, so great has *their* anxiety become, I can spare myself little sleep.

Now there is only one man I love to kiss when he is unshaven. Heterosexuality! you are inexorably approaching. (How discourage her?)

St. Serapion, I wrap myself in the robes of your whiteness which is like midnight in Dostoevsky. How am I to become a legend, my dear? I've tried love, but that hides you in the bosom of another and I am always springing forth from it like the lotus—the ecstasy of always bursting forth! (but one must not be distracted by it!) or like a hyacinth, "to keep the filth of life away," yes, there, even in the heart, where the filth is pumped in and slanders and pollutes and determines. I will my will, though I may become famous for a mysterious vacancy in that department, that greenhouse.

Destroy yourself, if you don't know!

It is easy to be beautiful; it is difficult to appear so. I admire you, beloved, for the trap you've set. It's like a final chapter no one reads because the plot is over.

"Fanny Brown is run away—scampered off with a
Cornet of Horse; I do love that little Minx, & hope She
may be happy, tho' She has vexed me by this Exploit a
little too. —Poor silly Cecchina! or F: B: as we used to
call her. —I wish She had a good Whipping and 10,000
pounds." —Mrs. Thrale.

I've got to get out of here. I choose a piece of shawl and
my dirtiest suntans. I'll be back, I'll re-emerge, defeated,
from the valley; you don't want me to go where you go,
so I go where you don't want me to. It's only afternoon,
there's a lot ahead. There won't be any mail downstairs.
Turning, I spit in the lock and the knob turns.

For James Dean

Welcome me, if you will,
as the ambassador of a hatred
who knows its cause
and does not envy you your whim
of ending him.

For a young actor I am begging
peace, gods. Alone
in the empty streets of New York
I am its dirty feet and head
and he is dead.

He has banged into your wall
of air, your hubris, racing
towards your heights and you
have cut him from your table
which is built, how unfairly
for us! not on trees, but on clouds.

I speak as one whose filth
is like his own, of pride
and speed and your terrible
example nearer than the siren's speech,
a spirit eager for the punishment
which is your only recognition.

Peace! to be true to a city
of rats and to love the envy
of the dreary, smudged mouthers

of an arcane dejection
smoldering quietly in the perception
of hopelessness and scandal
at unnatural vigor. Their dreams
are their own, as are the toilets
of a great railway terminal
and the sequins of a very small,
very fat eyelid.
     I take this
for myself, and you take up
the thread of my life between your teeth,
tin thread and tarnished with abuse,
you still shall hear
as long as the beast in me maintains
its taciturn power to close my lids
in tears, and my loins move yet
in the ennobling pursuit of all the worlds
you have left me alone in, and would be
the dolorous distraction from,
while you summon your army of anguishes
which is a million hooting blood vessels
on the eyes and in the ears
at that instant before death.
       And
the menials who surrounded him critically,
languorously waiting for a
final impertinence to rebel
and enslave him, starlets and other
glittering things in the hog-wallow,
lunging mireward in their inane
moth-like adoration of niggardly
cares and stagnant respects

paid themselves, you spared,
as a hospital preserves its orderlies.
Are these your latter-day saints,
these unctuous starers, muscular
somnambulists, these stages for which
no word's been written hollow
enough, these exhibitionists in
well-veiled booths, these navel-suckers?

Is it true that you high ones, celebrated
among amorous flies, hated the
prodigy and invention of his nerves?
To withhold your light
from painstaking paths!
your love
should be difficult, as his was hard.

Nostrils of pain down avenues
of luminous spit-globes breathe in
the fragrance of his innocent flesh
like smoke, the temporary lift,
the post-cancer excitement
of vile manners and veal-thin lips,
obscure in the carelessness of your scissors.

Men cry from the grave while they still live
and now I am this dead man's voice,
stammering, a little in the earth.
I take up
the nourishment of his pale green eyes,
out of which I shall prevent
flowers from growing, your flowers.

Sleeping on the Wing

Perhaps it is to avoid some great sadness,
as in a Restoration tragedy the hero cries "Sleep!
O for a long sound sleep and so forget it!"
that one flies, soaring above the shoreless city,
veering upward from the pavement as a pigeon
does when a car honks or a door slams, the door
of dreams, life perpetuated in parti-colored loves
and beautiful lies all in different languages.

Fear drops away too, like the cement, and you
are over the Atlantic. Where is Spain? where is
who? The Civil War was fought to free the slaves,
was it? A sudden down-draught reminds you of gravity
and your position in respect to human love. But
here is where the gods are, speculating, bemused.
Once you are helpless, you are free, can you believe
that? Never to waken to the sad struggle of a face?
to travel always over some impersonal vastness,
to be out of, forever, neither in nor for!

The eyes roll asleep as if turned by the wind
and the lids flutter open slightly like a wing.
The world is an iceberg, so much is invisible!
and was and is, and yet the form, it may be sleeping
too. Those features etched in the ice of someone
loved who died, you are a sculptor dreaming of space
and speed, your hand alone could have done this.
Curiosity, the passionate hand of desire. Dead,
or sleeping? Is there speed enough? And, swooping,

you relinquish all that you have made your own,
the kingdom of your self sailing, for you must awake
and breathe your warmth in this beloved image
whether it's dead or merely disappearing,
as space is disappearing and your singularity.

Radio

Why do you play such dreary music
on Saturday afternoon, when tired
mortally tired I long for a little
reminder of immortal energy?
                                        All
week long while I trudge fatiguingly
from desk to desk in the museum
you spill your miracles of Grieg
and Honegger on shut-ins.
                                        Am I not
shut in too, and after a week
of work don't I deserve Prokofieff?

Well, I have my beautiful de Kooning
to aspire to. I think it has an orange
bed in it, more than the ear can hold.

On Seeing Larry Rivers'
"Washington Crossing the Delaware"
at the Museum of Modern Art

Now that our hero has come back to us
in his white pants and we know his nose
trembling like a flag under fire,
we see the calm cold river is supporting
our forces, the beautiful history.

To be more revolutionary than a nun
is our desire, to be secular and intimate
as, when sighting a redcoat, you smile
and pull the trigger. Anxieties
and animosities, flaming and feeding

on theoretical considerations and
the jealous spiritualities of the abstract,
the robot? they're smoke, billows above
the physical event. They have burned up.
See how free we are! as a nation of persons.

Dear father of our country, so alive
you must have lied incessantly to be
immediate, here are your bones crossed
on my breast like a rusty flintlock,
a pirate's flag, bravely specific

and ever so light in the misty glare
of a crossing by water in winter to a shore

other than that the bridge reaches for.
Don't shoot until, the white of freedom glinting
on your gun barrel, you see the general fear.

For Janice and Kenneth to Voyage

Love, love, love,
honeymoon isn't used much in poetry these days

and if I give you a bar
of Palmolive Soap
it would be rather cracker-barrel
of me, wouldn't it?

The winds will wash you out your hair, my dears.
Passions will become turrets, to you.

I'll be so afraid
without you.
The penalty of the Big Town
is the Big Stick,

yet when you were laughing nearby
the monsters ignored me like a record-player

and I felt brilliant
to be so confident
that the trees
would walk back to Birnam Wood.

It was all you, your graceful white smiles
like a French word, the one for nursery, the one for brine.

Mayakovsky

My heart's aflutter!
I am standing in the bath tub
crying. Mother, mother
who am I? If he
will just come back once
and kiss me on the face
his coarse hair brush
my temple, it's throbbing!

then I can put on my clothes
I guess, and walk the streets.

2

I love you. I love you,
but I'm turning to my verses
and my heart is closing

like a fist.
Words! be
sick as I am sick, swoon,
roll back your eyes, a pool,
and I'll stare down
at my wounded beauty
which at best is only a talent
for poetry.

Cannot please, cannot charm or win
what a poet!
and the clear water is thick

with bloody blows on its head.
I embraced a cloud,
but when I soared
it rained.

3

That's funny! there's blood on my chest
oh yes, I've been carrying bricks
what a funny place to rupture!
and now it is raining on the ailanthus
as I step out onto the window ledge
the tracks below me are smoky and
glistening with a passion for running
I leap into the leaves, green like the sea

4

Now I am quietly waiting for
the catastrophe of my personality
to seem beautiful again,
and interesting, and modern.

The country is grey and
brown and white in trees,
snows and skies of laughter
always diminishing, less funny
not just darker, not just grey.

It may be the coldest day of
the year, what does he think of
that? I mean, what do I? And if I do,
perhaps I am myself again.